Inspiring Quotes
on
Creativity, Wisdom, and Spirituality

Mark-Gerard Keenan

Table of Contents

Foreword

Over 250 quotations are listed from famous personalities, artists, musicians, writers, scientists, philosophers, heroes, saints and sages. These provide a fascinating insight into living a creative, inspirational, truthful, successful and God-conscious life.

Additional quotes from the Christian scriptures, and from ancient Vedic scriptures, touch the soul, and help to purify our lives toward a higher spiritual path. This ultimately involves a relationship with God. The final chapters contain quotes from ancient Vedic texts on wisdom, truth, and spiritual life.

Included also are quotations from the ancient writings of 'Sri Canakya Pandit' who attained lasting fame some 2300 years ago for the effective guidance he gave to King Chandragupta Maurya. King Chandragupta defeated the famous Greek conqueror Alexander the Great. Canakya Pandit's most famous work *Niti Shastra* is variously translated as "the science of morality", "common sense", "expediency" or "ethics". The quotations contain ancient wisdom for modern success, and can be applied in many situations in our daily lives.

All Glories to God the source of all creativity, energy, and life itself.

Best wishes

Mark-Gerard Keenan

Life, Focus, Self Worth, and Success

"To keep the body in good health is a duty… Otherwise we will not be able to keep our mind strong and clear." – Buddha

"In the absence of purpose life becomes an endless journey to nowhere." – Seneca the Younger

"There is only one way to avoid criticism: do nothing, say nothing, and be nothing."- Aristotle

"Look for three things in a person – intelligence, energy, and integrity. If they don't have the last one, don't even bother with the first two." – Warren Buffet

"A man who lacks purpose distracts himself with pleasure" – Anonymous

"There are three solutions to every problem: accept it, change it, or leave it. Of you can't accept it, change it. If you can't change it, leave it." – Anonymous

"Don't blame a clown for acting like a clown. Ask yourself why you keep going to the circus." – Anonymous

"I learned long ago, never to wrestle with a pig. You get dirty, and besides, the pig likes it. " – George Bernard Shaw

"Never argue with stupid people, they will drag you down to their level and then beat you with experience." – Mark Twain

"A man without discipline is like a ship without a rudder drifting aimlessly." – Stoic insight

"The measure of a man is what he does with power." – Plato

"Fear is a reaction, courage is a decision." - Gina Rodriguez

"If you expect the world to be fair with you because you are fair, you're fooling yourself. That's like expecting the lion not to eat you because you did'nt eat him." – Anonymous

"Standing up for yourself doesn't make you argumentative. Sharing your feelings doesn't make you oversensitive. Saying no doesn't make you uncaring or selfish. If someone won't respect your feelings, needs and boundaries, the problem isn't you; it's them." – Anonymous

"I don't really care so much what people say about me because it usually is a reflection of who they are. For example, if people wish I would sound like I used to sound, then it says more about them than it does me." Prince, Famous Musician

"Cool means being able to hang with yourself. All you have to ask yourself is 'Is there anybody I`m afraid of? Is there anybody who if I walked into a room and saw, I`d get nervous?' If not, then you`re cool." - Prince, Famous Musician

"A strong spirit transcends rules." - Prince, Famous Musician

"Sometimes it takes years for a person to become an overnight success." - Prince, Famous Musician

"Money won't buy you happiness, but it'll pay for the search" - Prince, Famous Musician

"When I want to hear new music, I make it." - Prince, Famous Musician

"If you see a man opening a car door for a woman, it means one of two things: it's either a new woman or a new car!" - Prince, Famous Musician

"Conquer yourself rather than the world." – Rene Descartes

"You need to claim the events of your life to make yourself yours." – Anne-Wilson Schaef

"Do not correct a fool or he will hate you, correct a wise man and he will appreciate you." – Bruce Lee

"An affirmation is a strong positive statement that something is already so." – Sharti Gawain

"Go confidently in the direction of your dreams! Live the life you've imagined. As you simplify your life, the laws of the universe will be simpler." – Henry David Thoreau

"Make your own recovery the first priority in your life." – Robin Norwood

"Snipers are people who understand your efforts to break unhealthy relationship patterns." Jody Hayes

"To know what you prefer instead of humbly saying Amen to what the world tells you ought to prefer, is to have kept your soul alive." – Robert Louis Stevenson

"Every time you don't follow your inner guidance, you feel a loss of energy, loss of power, a sense of spiritual deadness." – Shakti Gawain

"Slow down and enjoy life. It's not only the scenery you miss by going too fast – you also miss the sense of where you are going and why." – Eddie Cantor

"Chance is always powerful. Let your hook be always cast; in the pool where you last expect it, there will be a fish." - Ovid

"Did you ever observe to whom the accidents happen? Chance favors only the prepared mind." - Louis Pasteur

"The cost of a thing is the amount of what I call life which is required to be exchanged for it, immediately or in the long run." – Henry David

Thoreau

"What does'nt kill me makes me stronger. " – Albert Camus

"Take your life in your own hands and what happens? A terrible thing; no one to blame." – Erica Jong

"Surround yourself with people who respect and treat you well." – Claudia Black

"Trust that still, small voice that says, "this might work and I'll try it." – Diana Mariechild

"Man can learn nothing except by going from the known to the unknown." – Claude Bernard

"Saying no can be the ultimate self-care." – Claudia Black

"… our lives are all that really belong to us. So it is how we use our lives that determines the kind of men we are." – Cesar Chavez

"He who knows others is wise; he who knows himself is enlightened." – Lao-Tzu

"A funny thing about life; if you refuse to accept anything but the best, you very often get it." – Somerset Maugham

Artists, Writers, and Musicians on Creativity and God

"Every day I feel is a blessing from God. And I consider it a new beginning. Yeah, everything is beautiful." – Prince, famous Musician

"My God is real" – Johnny Cash

"I myself do nothing. The Holy Spirit accomplishes all through me." – William Blake, Poet

"In the brush doing what it is doing; it will stumble on what one could'nt do by oneself." – Robert Motherwell

"The position of the artist is humble. He is essentially a channel." – Piet Mondrian

"The music of this opera [Madame Butterfly] was dictated to me by God; I was merely instrumental in putting it on paper and communicating it to the public." – Giacomo Puccini

"Straightaway the ideas flow in upon me, directly from God." – Johannes

Brahms

"We must accept that this creative pulse within us is God's creative pulse itself." – Joseph Chilton Pearce

"What we play is life." – Louis Armstrong

"I paint not be sight but by faith. Faith gives you sight." – Amos Ferguson

"Why should we all use our creative power…? Because there is nothing that makes people so generous, joyful, lively, bold, and compassionate, so indifferent to fighting and the accumulation of objects and money." – Brenda Ueland

"The purpose of art is not a rarified, intellectual distillate – it is life, intensified, brilliant life." – Alain Arias-Mission

"What lies behind us and what lies before us are tiny matters, compared to what lies within us." – Ralph Waldo Emerson

"Inspiration may be a form of superconsciousness, or perhaps of subconsciousness – I would'nt know. But I am sure it is the anti-thesis of self-consciousness." – Aaron Copland

"Like an ability or a muscle, hearing your inner wisdom is strengthened by doing it." – Robbie Gass

"Painting is just another way of keeping a diary." – Pablo Picasso

"At the height of laughter, the universe is flung into a kaleidoscope of new possibilities." – Jean Houston

"Every child is an artist. The problem is how to remain an artist once he grows up." – Pablo Picasso

"The unconscious wants truth. It ceases to speak to those who want something else more than truth." – Adrienne Rich

"During these periods of relaxation after concentrated intellectual activity, the intuitive mind seems to take over and can produce the sudden clarifying insights which give so much joy and delight." – Fritjof Capra, Physicist

"Younger Self – who can be as balky and stubborn as the most cantankerous three-year-old – is not impressed by words. Like a native of Missouri, it wants to be shown. To arouse its interest, we must seduce it with pretty pictures and pleasurable sensations – take it out dining and dancing as it were. Only in this way can Deep Self be reached." – Starhawk Theologian

"To live a creative life, we must lose our fear of being wrong." – Joseph Chilton Pearce

"When you are feeling deprecated angry or drained it is a sign that other people are not open to your energy." – Sanaya Roman

"Painting is an attempt to come to terms with life. There are as many solutions are there are human beings." – George Tooker

"I cannot believe that the inscrutable universe turns on an axis of suffering; surely the strange beauty of the world must somewhere rest on pure joy!" – Louise Bogan

"The meeting of two personalities is like the contact of two chemical substances: if there is any reaction, both are transformed." – C.G. Jung

"Whatever God's dream about man may be, it seems it cannot come true unless man co-operates." – Stella Terill Mann

"Think of yourself as an incandescent power, illuminated and perhaps forvever talked to by God and his messengers." – Brenda Ueland

"The flashpoint of creation in the present moment is where work and play merge." – Stephen Nachmanovitch

"The painting has a life of its own. I try to let it come through." – Jackson Pollock

"I shut my eyes in order to see. " – Paul Gauguin

"I merely took the energy it takes to pout and wrote some blues." – Duke Ellington

"There is a vitality, a life force, an energy, a quickening, that is translated through you into action, and because there is only one of you in all time, this expression is unique. And if you block it, it will never exist through any other medium and will be lost." – Martha Graham

"Creativity is… seeing something that does'nt exist already. You need to find out how you can bring it into being and that way be a playmate with God." – Michele Shea

"Stop thinking and talking about it and there is nothing you will not be able to know." – Zen paradigm

"It is not because things are difficult that we do not dare; it is because we do not dare that they are difficult." – Seneca

"I learned that the real creator was my inner Self, the Shakti… That desire to do something is God inside talking through us." – Michele Shea

"Look and you will find it – what is unsought will go undetected." – Sophocles

"It is in my power either to serve God or not serve him. Serving him, I add to my own good and the good of the whole world. Not serving him, I forfeit my own good and deprive the world of that good, which was in my power to create." – Leo Tolstoy

"Often people attempt to live their lives backwards: they try to have more things, or more money, in order to do more of what they want so that they will be happier. The way it actually works is the reverse. You must first be who you really are, then, do what you need to do, in order to have what you want." – Margaret Young

"To accept the responsibility of being a child of God is to accept that best that life has to offer you." – Stella Terill Mann

"Money is God in action." – Raymond Charles Barker

"The more we learn to operate in the world based on trust in our intuition, the stronger our channel will be and the more money we will have." – Shakti Gawain

"Explore daily the will of God." – C. G. Jung

"Celebration is the enemy of originality in art." – Martin Ritt

"Living is a form of not being sure, not knowing what next or how. The moment you know how, you begin to die a little. The artist never entirely knows. We guess. We may be wrong, but we take leap after leap in the dark." Agnes de Mille

"Take a risk a day – one small or bold stroke that will make you feel great once you have done it." – Susan Jeffers

"Shoot for the moon. Even if you miss it you will land among the stars." - Les Brown

"I am in the world only for the purpose of composing." – Franz Schubert

"Your desire is your prayer. Picture the fulfilment of your desire now and feel its reality and you will experience the joy of the answered prayer." – Dr. Joseph Murphy

"Art evokes the mystery without which the world would not exist." – Rene- Francois Ghislain Magritte

"Life shrinks or expands in proportion to one's courage." – Anais Nin

"Do not fear mistakes there are none" - Miles Davis

"One does not discover new lands without consenting to lose sight of the shore for a very long time." – Andre Gide

"Creation is only the projection into form of that which already exists." – Srimad Bhagavatam, Ancient Vedic Text

"A painting is never finished it simply stops in interesting places." – Paul Gardner

"I learn by going where I have to go." – Theodore Roethke

Scientists that Realised the Existence of God

"Overwhelming strong proofs of intelligent and benevolent design lie around us. The atheistic idea is so nonsensical that I cannot put it into word" – Lord Kelvin, the scientific father of thermodynamics

"Those who say that the study of science makes a man an atheist must be rather silly people" – Physics Noble Laureate Max Born

"There is no incompatibility between science and religion. Science proves that God exists. " – Chemistry Noble Laureate Derek Barton

"When I examine the orderliness, understandability, and beauty of the universe, I am led to the conclusion that a higher intelligence designed what I see. My scientific appreciation of the coherence, the delightful simplicity, of physics strengthens my belief in God... a God who is both the creator of the universe and is ultimately concerned with the welfare of the creatures of that universe.... I believe that scientific research is a deeply religious calling" - William D. Phillips, Nobel Laureate in Physics, University of Maryland

"An equation for me has no meaning, unless it represents a thought of God." – Ramanujan, Famous mathematics genius

"The universe has been brought for us by a supremely good and orderly creator" – Nicholas Copernicus

"For a person whose spiritual orientation is in the framework of a supreme benevolent entity, the world is the handiwork of that entity. The study of the intricacies and beauty of the world is an act of devotion. Pursuing science becomes an act of worship... Contemporary science looks at the world in terms of utility (technology and standard of life)... But never does it aim to see uninterrupted happiness as the aim of all disciplines... " – E.C. G Sudarshan, Particle Physicist, University of Texas

"I saw in it (the atom) the key to the deepest secret of nature, and it revealed to me the greatness of the creation and the Creator." – Max Born, one of the pioneers of quantum physics

"Although 2,000 years of Aristotelian worldview maintained that insects are devoid of any internal organs, Swammerdam showed that they are as complex as the large mammals. For him the source of this artistic design, complexity and natural order could only be divine, and his only response was rapture." - Dr T. D. Singh PhD referring to the work of Dutch anatomist and pioneer microscopist Jan Swammerdam (1637-80)

"I find that existence can no more be separated from the essence of God than from the essence of a rectilinear triangle can be separated the equality of its three angles to two right angles, or, indeed, if you please, from the idea of a mountain the idea of a valley" – Descartes

"I am convinced of the afterlife, independent of theology. If the world is rationally constructed, there must be an afterlife" – Kurt Gödel, Famous mathematician

"I think only an idiot can be an atheist" – Christan B. Anfinsen, Noble Laureate chemist

"Little science takes you away from God but more of it takes you to him"
– Louis Pasteur, Founder of Microbiology

"All things are indeed contrived and ordered with singular providence, divine wisdom, and most admirable and incomprehensible skill. And to none can these attributes be referred save to the Almighty." – Sir William Harvey, Founder of Modern Medicine

"For me the idea of a creation is inconceivable without God. One cannot be exposed to the law and order of the universe without concluding that there must be a divine intent behind it all." – Werner Von Braun, Founder of Astronautics

"We feed our bodies; our Souls are also to be fed: The Food of the Soul is Knowledge, especially Knowledge in the Things of God," – John Ray, Founder of Modern Biology

"When I reflect on so many profoundly marvelous things that persons have grasped, sought, and done, I recognize even more clearly that human intelligence is a work of God, and one of the most excellent" - Galileo Galilei, Founder of Experimental Physics

"There are two books laid before us to study, to prevent our failing into error, the first, the volume of Scriptures, which reveal the will of God; then the volume of the creatures, which express His power." - Sir Francis Bacon, Founder of the Scientific Inductive Method

"Little science takes you away from God but more of it takes you to him"
– Louis Pasteur, Founder of Microbiology

"For me the idea of a creation is inconceivable without God. One cannot be exposed to the law and order of the universe without concluding that there must be a divine intent behind it all." – Wemher Von Braun, Founder of Astronautics

"And thus, I very clearly see that the certitude and truth of all science depends on the knowledge alone of the true God, insomuch that, before I knew him, I could have no perfect knowledge of any other thing." – Rene Descartes, Founder of Analytical Geometry

"We ought to value the privilege of knowing God's truth far beyond anything we can have in this world" – Michael Faraday, Scientist

"If we think deep enough, we can realize that there can be no one other than God who can (i) impart perfect order and majestic beauty in nature (ii) make the physical laws of nature, (iii) manifest the wonderful world of myriad of living beings." - Dr T. D. Singh PhD

"In God there is Power, which is the source of all, also Knowledge, whose content is the variety of the ideas, and finally Will, which makes change or products according to the principle of the best." – Wilhelm Leibniz, Founder of Infinitesimal Calculus

"There are two books laid before us to study, to prevent our failing into error, the first, the volume of Scriptures, which reveal the will of God; then the volume of the creatures, which express His power." - Sir Francis Bacon, Founder of the Scientific Inductive Method

"I believe in God. It makes no sense to me to assume that the Universe and our existence is just a cosmic accident, that life emerged due to random physical processes in an environment which simply happened to have the right properties." – Antony Hewish, 1974 Nobel in Physics

"The more we learn about creation – the way it emerged – it just adds to the glory of God." – Joseph Murray, Nobel Laureate in Medicine and Physiology

"For religion, God is at the beginning; for science, God is at the end." – Max Planck, Nobel Laureate in Physics

"There is a higher power, not influenced by our wishes, which finally decides and judges." – Werner Heisenberg, 1932-Nobel Laureate in Physics

"I have endeavoured to gain for human reason, aided by geometrical calculation, an insight into His way of creation... may He cause us to aspire to the perfection of His works of creation by the dedication of our lives..." – Johannes Kepler, Founder of physical astronomy

"Almighty God, who has created man in Thine own image, and made him a living soul that he might seek after Thee, and have dominion over Thy creatures, teach us to study the works of Thy hands, that we may subdue the earth to our use, and strengthen the reason for Thy service." – James Clerk Maxwell, Founder of statistical Thermodynamics

"Those to whom God has imparted religion by intuition are very fortunate and justly convinced. But to those who do not have it, we can give it only by reasoning, waiting for God to give them spiritual insight." – Blaise Pascal

"Through steady observation and a meaningful contact with the divined Order of the world's structure, arranged by God's wisdom, - who would not be guided to admire the Builder who creates all!" – Copernicus

"Overwhelming evidences of an intelligence and benevolent intention surround us, show us the whole of nature through the work of a free will and teach us that all alive beings depend on an eternal creator-ruler." – Lord Kelvin, Founder of thermodynamics

"For me, faith begins with the realization that a supreme intelligence brought the universe into being and created man. It is not difficult for me to have this faith, for an orderly, intelligent universe testifies to the greatest statement ever uttered: 'In the beginning, God… " – Arthur Campton

"The principle of divine purpose… stares the biologist in the face wherever he looks… The probability for such an event as the origin of DNA molecules to have occurred by sheer chance is just too small to be seriously considered." – Ernest Boris Chain, Nobel Laureate in medicine

"When confronted with the marvels of life and the universe, one must ask why the only possible answers are religious… I find a need for God in the universe and in my own life." – Arthur L. Schawlow, Nobel Laureate in physics

"The more I work with the powers of Nature, the more I feel God's benevolence to man." – Guglielmo Marconi, 1909, Nobel Prize in Physics

"I maintain that the human mystery is incredibly demeaned by scientific reductionism, with its claim in promissory materialism to account eventually for all the spiritual world in terms of patterns of neuronal activity. This belief must be classed as a superstition… We have to recognize that we are spiritual beings with souls existing in a spiritual world as a material beings with bodies and brains existing in a material world" – John Eccles, Brain Researcher

Inspiration, Conscience, Consciousness, and the Soul

"It is by logic we prove, it is by intuition that we invent, … Logic, therefore, remains barren unless fertilised by intuition." – Henry Poincare, Famous Mathematician and Physicist

"The mind can proceed only so far upon what it knows and can prove. There comes a point where the mind takes a higher plane of knowledge, but can never prove how it got there. All great discoveries have involved such a leap." – Einstein (see also my book *Godless Fake Science* for some interesting commentary on Mr. Einstein)

"We can admittedly find nothing in physics or chemistry that has even a remote bearing on consciousness. Yet all of us know that there is such a thing as consciousness, simply because we have it ourselves. Hence consciousness must be art of nature, or, more generally, of reality, which means that, quite apart from the laws of physics and chemistry… we must consider laws of quite a different kind." – Niels Bohr, 1922 Nobel Laureate, Physics

"It is a fact that there is a point, one single point in the immeasurable expanse of mind and matter, where science and therefore every causal method research is inapplicable, not only on practical grounds, but also on logical grounds, and will always remain inapplicable. This is the point of [our] individual awareness." – Max Planck, Physicist

"The evidence is coming in from all sides: that physics and chemistry cannot account for more than a kind of substratum of phenomena and must be seen as being in the service of higher forces when it comes to matters like life, intelligence and consciousness" – E. F. Schumacher, Author

"The scientific community practices the art of 'refusal of consciousness' with perfection… survival will depend on our ability to overcome the 'refusal of consciousness' which defends totally outdated philosophies of economic progress and scientific truth" – E.F. Schumacher, Author

"We have discovered ourselves to be in a very, very deep spiritual crisis. An era which has been dominated by cartesian thinking and which has lasted for 250 or 300 years, has seen unbelievable developments in science and technology. This era is now drawing to a close. Having worked out the consequences of this type of thinking we find ourselves spiritually bankrupt." – E.F. Schumacher

"I think that in this century, science will be admitted to the spiritual aspects of mankind, and vice versa – what has been segregated for at least 300 hundred years, since Galileo" – Professor Karl H. Pribham, Distinguished Research Professor, Georgetown University, Professor Emeritus, Stanford and Radford Universities

"Krishna [God] is continuously transmitting guidance from within. Unfortunately, the clamour of desires for materialistic pleasure deafens us to His voice. When we silence these desires and tune our heart to His receiving frequency, then the receiving antenna of our heart can receive His signals. We can tune ourselves by the process of devotional service, as confirmed in the Bhagavad Gita… " – Chaitanya Charon Das, Author

"the stream of knowledge is heading toward a non-mechanical reality; the Universe begins to look more like a great thought than like a great machine. Mind no longer appears to be an accidental intruder into the realm of matter… we ought rather hail it as the creator and governor of the realm of matter." – Richard Conn Henry, Professor of Physics, John Hopkins University

"I maintain that the human mystery is incredibly demeaned by scientific reductionism, with its claim in promissory materialism to account eventually for all of the spiritual world in terms of patterns of neuronal activity. This belief must be classed as superstition… we have to recognize that we are spiritual beings with souls existing in a spiritual world as well as material beings with bodies and brains"- John Eccles, Nobel Laureate in Medicine and Physiology

"He who is not angry when there is just cause for anger is immoral. Why? Because anger looks to the good of justice. And if you can live amid injustice without anger, you are immoral as well as unjust." – Thomas Aquinas, Priest, Philosopher (pictured below)

"James 1:5. If any of you lacks wisdom, let him ask God, who gives generously to all without reproach, and it will be given him." – Christian Bible

"Proverbs 1:7. The fear of the Lord is the beginning of knowledge; fools despise wisdom and instruction." - Christian Bible

"do you think that you can take over the universe and improve it - I do not believe it can be done – everything under heaven is a sacred vessel and cannot be controlled – trying to control leads to ruin - trying to grasp we lose - allow your life to unfold naturally, know that it too is a vessel of perfection' 'to the sage all of life is a movement toward perfection" - from the 29th verse Tao Te Ching

Society, Truth, Politics, Conformity, Propaganda, and Freedom

"No face which we can give to a matter will stead us so well at last as the truth. This alone wears well… Say what you have to say, not what you ought. Any truth is better than make-believe." - Henry David Thoreau

"Rather than love, than money, than fame, give me truth. I sat at a table where were rich food and wine in abundance, and obsequious attendance, but sincerity and truth were not; and I went away hungry from the inhospitable board. " – Henry David Thoreau

"As if there were safety in stupidity alone." – Henry David Thoreau

"By truth the earth is sustained. By truth the sun shines, and Truth causes Vayu the wind god to blow. Verily all things rest upon truth." – Sri Canakya Niti (Sloka 5.19), Ancient Vedic Text

"Let us settle ourselves, and work and wedge our feet downward through the mud and slush of opinion, and prejudice, and tradition, and delusion, and appearance, that alluvion which covers the globe, through Paris and London, through New York and Boston and Concord, through Church and State, through poetry and philosophy and religion, till we come to a hard bottom and rocks in place, which we can call reality, and say, This is, and no mistake"- Henry David Thoreau

"If you stand right fronting and face to face to a fact, you will see the sun glimmer on both its surfaces, as if it were a cimeter, [scimitar: a curved sword] and feel its sweet edge dividing you through the heart and marrow, and so you will happily conclude your mortal career. Be it life or death, we crave only reality." – Henry David Thoreau

"All truth passes through three stages. First, it is ridiculed. Second, it is violently opposed. Third, it is accepted as being self-evident." – Arthur Schopenhauer

"The more wisdom you attain, the crazier you seem to the unaware and indoctrinated." – Anonymous

"He who dares not offend cannot be honest" – Thomas Paine

"No one is more hated than he who speaks the truth." – Plato

"It is easier to fool people than convince them they have been fooled." – Anonymous

"The highest truth is reality distinguished from illusion for the welfare of all" - The ancient text, the Srimad Bhagavatam Sloka 1.1.2., written in Sanskrit over 5,000 years ago and translated into English by His Divine Grace A.C. Bhaktivedanta Srila Prabhupada.

"Freedom is the sure possession of those alone who have the courage to defend it." – Pericles

"What if I told you the left wing and the right wing below to the same bird." – Anonymous

"We live in a time where intelligent people are being silenced so that stupid people won't be offended." – Anonymous

"They fear love because it creates a world they can't control." – George Orwell, 1984

"Most people spend over a decade at school during crucial formative years being told what to think, what to speak, what to write, and what to read. Is it really any surprise why critical thinking is a skill so rarely observed today? " – Anonymous

"Once you understand that they are not journalists and media professionals, but, rather, actors and operatives, things will start to make sense." - Anonymous

"He who cannot obey himself will be commanded." - Nietzsche

"You are only rebellious in the eyes of those who cannot manipulate or control you." – Anonymous

"The deep critical thinker has become the misfit of the world, this is not a co-incidence. To maintain order and control you must isolate the intellectual, the sage, the philosopher, the savant before their ideas awaken people." – Carl Gustav Jung

"We don't let society show us how its supposed to be... " - Prince, Famous Musician

"Sometimes people don't want to hear the truth because they don't want their illusions destroyed." – Friedrich Nietzche

"If the news is fake, imagine how bad history is." – Anonymous

"Conformity is doing what everybody else is doing, regardless of what is right. Morality is doing what is right, regardless of what everybody is doing." - Evette Carter

"It is hard to free fools from the chains they revere." – Voltaire

"Manipulation is when they blame you for your reaction to their disrespect." – Anonymous

"When the state does everything for you, it will soon take everything away from you." – Margeret Thatcher

"I would rather have questions that can't be answered, than answers that can't be questioned" – Richard Feynman

"Government is the ridiculous idea that some people can have the moral right to rule everyone else and make it okay for them to boss around the sectors of population under threat of force… the idea that we need to give a group of people (governments) permission to forcibly rob us (via taxes) and control us (via government restrictions and huge police forces) so that they can protect us from those few private individuals who might possibly in the future forcibly rob and control us is ridiculous" - Anonymous

"All we need is the right major crisis and the nations will accept the new world order" – David Rockefeller

"You have to understand, most of these people are not ready to be unplugged. And many of them are so inured, so hopelessly dependent on the system, that they will fight to protect it." – from the movie' The Matrix'

"If you don't shape your own mind the system will gladly shape it for you." – Anonymous

"Football, beer, and above all, gambling filled up the horizon of their minds. To keep them in control was not difficult." – George Orwell, 1984

The war is not meant to be won it is meant to be continuous." – George Orwell

"However much you deny the truth the truth goes on existing" – George Orwell

"Sometimes the black sheep of the family is the only one who has the balls to tell the truth" – Anonymous

"Success is not the key to happiness. Happiness is the key to success." – Albert Schweitzer

"One idiot is one idiot. Two idiots are two idiots. Ten thousand idiots are a political party." – Franz Kafka

"The people who currently own this world don't care which ruler you choose. They care only that you keep choosing to be ruled." – Anonymous

"Don't be too impressed by college degress anymore. Graduates are no longer the most educated. They're just the most indoctrinated."

"Keep in mind, the new media are not independent; they are a sort of bulletin board and public relations firm for the ruling classes – the people who run things. Those whose decide what news you will or will not hear are paid by, and tolerated purely at the whim of those who hold economic power. If the parent corporation does'nt want you to know something, it won't be on the news. Period. Or, at the very least, it will be slanted to suit them, and then rarely followed up." – George Carlin

See also the Reality Distinguished from Illusion website at **www.mkeenan.ie** for more information

Beyond Material Consciousness Toward the Joy of Spiritual Life

"And what is good, Phaedrus, And what is not good - Need we ask anyone to tell us these things?" - from *'Zen and the Art of Motorcycle Maintenance: An Inquiry Into Values'* by Robert Pirsig

"And now he began to see for the first time the unbelievable magnitude of what man when he gained power to understand and rule the world… had lost. He had built empires of scientific capability to manipulate the phenomena of nature into enormous manifestations of his owns dreams of power and wealth – but for this he had exchanged an empire of understanding of equal magnitude: an understanding of what it is to be part of the world, and not an enemy of it." – from *'Zen and the Art of Motorcycle Maintenance: An Inquiry Into Values'* by Robert Pirsig

".. the worst of faults is wanting more…always… When action is pure and selfless, everything settles into its own perfect place" – extract from the Tao Te Ching 7th verse by Lao Tzu (the Tao symbol is shown below)

"… temperantia, that is, the virtue of self-control, discipline and moderation, which preserves and defends order in the individual and in the environment – we can see that this is the virtue most needed and at the same time the virtue most conspicuous by its absence in the modern world.. ." – E.F. Schumacher

"He whose wealth is enjoyment must abandon any quest for knowledge. He who values knowledge must not desire sense gratification." – Sri Canakya niti (Sloka 10.3), Ancient Vedic Text

"One who is undisturbed by the flow of desires, as the ocean is unmoved by the incessant flow of rivers, finds peace." – Bhagavad Gita, 2.70, translation by Srila Prabhupada

"Completely rejecting all religious activities which are materially motivated, the Bhagavata Purana propounds the highest truth… The highest truth is reality distinguished from illusion for the welfare of all. Such truth uproots the threefold miseries." – Srimad Bhagavatam 1.1.2, translation by Srila Prabhupada, Ancient Vedic Text

"Because we see almost everyone around us pursuing material goals – sex, wealth, luxuries, prestige, power, fame – we assume such pursuits to be the natural purpose of life. But, as the saying goes, "Do not think you are on the right road just because its well-worn…." – Chaitanya Charan das, Author

"We have been born into ignorance in this world of temporary names and labels, which are simply shrouds of the soul… we are all helplessly torn apart by the currents of time… are forced to continue on our way according to the fate written in our stars at birth… For he who arrives at the lotus feet of the Lord, all miseries vanish in the spirit of bliss, even while living in this world of names." – Commentary on Sri Canakya niti (Sloka 10.15) by Patita Pavana Dasa Adhikari

"Most men, even in this comparatively free country, through mere ignorance and mistake, are so occupied with the factitious cares and superfluously coarse labors of life that its finer fruits cannot be plucked by them" - Henry David Thoreau, American Writer and Philosopher

"… a man is rich in proportion to the number of things which he can afford to let alone." - Henry David Thoreau, American Writer and Philosopher

"If they had not been overcome with drowsiness, they would have performed something. The millions are awake enough for physical labor; but only one in a million is awake enough for effective intellectual exertion, only one in a hundred millions to a poetic or divine life." – Henry David Thoreau, American Writer and Philosopher

"We must learn to reawaken and keep ourselves awake, not by mechanical aids, but by an infinite expectation of the dawn, which does not forsake us in our soundest sleep. I know of no more encouraging fact than the unquestionable ability of man to elevate his life by a conscious endeavor" – Henry David Thoreau, American Writer and Philosopher

"Men think that it is essential that the Nation have commerce, and export ice, and talk through a telegraph, and ride thirty miles an hour, without a doubt, whether they do or not; but whether we should live like baboons or like men, is a little uncertain…" – Henry David Thoreau, American Writer and Philosopher

"And I am sure that I never read any memorable news in a newspaper…If you are acquainted with the principle, what do you care for a myriad instances and applications? To a philosopher all news, as it is called, is gossip, and they who edit and read it are old women over their tea." – Henry David Thoreau, American Writer and Philosopher

"By closing the eyes and slumbering, and consenting to be deceived by shows, men establish and confirm their daily life of routine and habit everywhere, which still is built on purely illusory foundations." – Henry David Thoreau, American Writer and Philosopher

"be a Columbus to whole new continents and worlds within you, opening new channels, not of trade, but of thought. Every man is the lord of a realm beside which the earthly empire of the Czar is but a petty state... Yet some… sacrifice the greater to the less. They love the soil which makes their graves, but have no sympathy with the spirit which may still animate their clay." – Henry David Thoreau, American Writer and Philosopher

"I learned this, at least, by my experiment: that if one advances confidently in the direction of his dreams, and endeavors to live the life which he has imagined, he will meet with a success unexpected in common hours. He will put some things behind, will pass an invisible boundary; new, universal, and more liberal laws will begin to establish themselves around and within him; or the old laws be expanded, and interpreted in his favor in a more liberal sense, and he will live with the license of a higher order of beings. In proportion as he simplifies his life, the laws of the universe will appear less complex, and solitude will not be solitude, nor poverty poverty, nor weakness weakness. If you have built castles in the air, your work need not be lost; that is where they should be. Now put the foundations under them." – Henry David Thoreau, American Writer and Philosopher

"Let everyone mind his own business, and endeavor to be what he was made. Why should we be in such desperate haste to succeed and in such desperate enterprises? If a man does not keep pace with his companions, perhaps it is because he hears a different drummer. Let him step to the music which he hears, however measured or far away." - Henry David Thoreau, American Writer and Philosopher

"… but to walk even with the Builder of the universe, if I may -- not to live in this restless, nervous, bustling, trivial Nineteenth Century, but stand or sit thoughtfully while it goes by. What are men celebrating? They are all on a committee of arrangements, and hourly expect a speech from somebody. God is only the president of the day" - Henry David Thoreau, American Writer and Philosopher

"Chess is ultimately a battle, a fight, a clash of egos. It is about winning, about defeating the other person. If you seriously adopt this attitude, and you inevitably have to as an international tournament player, you block your access to a higher spiritual path, to overcoming your ego, to finding and taking the next step. The world is not a chess board. It does not consist of 64 fields, half of them black, half of them white. As soon as you have truly understood this, there is no way you can spend your life playing games anymore, however complex they may be. Life is much more than a game and should be used to gain insight and knowledge as long as you live." – Marcus Schmieke, Author

"As a calf finds its mother among a thousand cows, so the [good or bad] deeds of a man follow him" – Sri Canakya niti (Sloka 3.14)

"Life's desires should never be directed toward sense gratification. One should desire only a healthy life, or self-preservation, since a human being is meant for inquiry about the Absolute Truth (Ultimate Reality). Nothing else should be the goal of one's works." – a verse from the Srimad Bhagavatam (S.B. 1.2.10)

A God-conscious Life and Society – the Words of Christian Saints and Notable Authors

"What do you have to fear? Nothing. Whom do you have to fear? No one. Why? Because whoever has joined forces with God obtains three great privileges: omnipotence without power, intoxication without wine, and life without death." – Francis of Assisi (statue pictured below), a Christian Saint

".. the service of mammon is not reward by lasting prosperity, but by cataclysmic disaster. It is the service of God – or of Truth, as Asia would say – that alone leads to lasting well-being on this earth... What we wish to do with our lives obviously depends first of all on what we think we are... What are we then - naked apes or a peculiar people to whom was given the power to become sons of God?" – E.F. Schumacher

'Love God with all your heart, and with all your soul, and with all your mind. This is the greatest and first commandment." - Matt. (22.37-40), Christian Bible

"After all, Jesus often said that he was only preaching what the Law and the prophets had taught long ago… I certainly won't claim that all religions are the same, but when so many have such common features, I find it hard to argue that the loving and personal God I experience is not at work in the hearts of those people of other faiths." - William D Phillips, Nobel Laureate in Physics, University of Maryland, describing his Christian faith

"The best you can do in the confrontation with evil forces is not to allow them to influence yet another person, namely you, as this would drag them even deeper into darkness…. When Satan came to seduce Jesus with an offer of global power, Jesus answered, 'Away with you, Satan!' This was not an expression of hate or fear but of unconditional love. Through this clear differentiation and demarcation Jesus protected Satan from falling into even deeper darkness." – Armin Risi, Author

"Obviously, 'do not judge' does not mean 'do not differentiate'! Jesus often differentiated very critically. Some men he even called 'fools and blind ones... snakes, broods of vipers. (Matt. 23.17,33)" - – Armin Risi, Author

"You must either conquer the world or the world will conquer you. You must be either master or slave." – St. John Henry Cardinal Newman, Christian

"Abandon yourself utterly for the love of God, and in this way you will become truly happy." – St. Henry Suso, Christian

"It is the highest duty of religion to imitate Him whom you adore." – St. Augustine of Hippo, Christian

"Let us work as if success depends on us alone, but with the heartfelt convictions that we are doing nothing and God everything." – St. Ignatius of Loyola, Christian

"Without work, it's impossible to have fun." – St. Thomas Aquinas, Christian

"I have started houses with *no* more than the price of a loaf of bread and prayers, for with Him who comforts me, I can do anything." – St. Frances Xavier Cabrini, Christian

"The more you abandon to God the care of all temporal things, the more He will take care to provide for all your wants; but if, on the contrary, you try to supply all your own needs, Providence will allow you to continue to do just that, and then it may very well happen that even necessities will be lacking, God thus reproving you for your lack of faith and reliance on him." – St. Jean-Baptist de La Salle, Christian

"Entrust yourself entirely to God. He is a Father and a most loving Father at that, who would rather let heaven and earth collapse than abandon anyone who trusted in him." – St. Paul of the Cross, Christian

"Do now – do *now* – what you'll wish you had done when your moment comes to die." – St. Angela Merici, Christian

"When death comes, the mighty messenger of God, no king can command him, no authority can restrain him, no riches can hire him to wait past his appointed time even one moment of an hour. Therefore, let us consider well in time what words we are bound to speak and what deeds we are bound to do, and let us say them and do them quickly. And let us leave unsaid and undone all superfluous things (and, much more, all damnable things), knowing well we have no empty time allowed us." – St. Thomas More, Christian

"… the inability of Westerners to interpret the east is bound up with their failure to penetrate the deeper meaning of their own sages and even of the Gospels. Reciprocally, it may be said that by a genuine assimilation of the essential content of the Eastern traditions, they might be helped to recapture the spirit that dwells at the heart of Christianity itself..." – E.F. Schumacher, Renowned Author

"What if I told you that waiting for Jesus to return is a deception to distract you from discovering Christ within you? What if I told you that who you are waiting on, is waiting for you?" – Anonymous

"Away with you Satan!" "Away from me Satan!" – The words of Jesus Christ when the devil tried to tempt Jesus (Matthew 4:10)

Wisdom from the Ancient Writings of 'Sri Canakya Pandit'

Shri Canakya Pandit attained lasting fame some 2300 years ago for his Snaskrit writings; and for the practical and effective counsel he gave to King Chandragupta Maurya (shown in the scultpure below) who conquered most of India under his guidance. In the process, the famous Greek conqueror Alexander the Great was defeated by King Chandragupta. Shri Canakya Pandit's most famous work *Niti Shastra* is variously translated as "the science of morality", "common sense", "expediency" or "ethics". The writings contain wisdom that may be applied to our daily lives.

"…make sure your enemy comes to grief, but engage your friends in spiritual life." – Sloka 3.3

"At the time of pralaya [universal destruction or death] the oceans exceed theor limits and seek to change. Yet saintly men, even at the time of pralaya, do not change." – Sloka 3.6

"Do not associate with a nincompoop [fool]…" – Sloka 3.7

"There can be no quarrel with someone who is silent. He who is vigilant cannot be overcome by fear." – Sloka 3.11

"He who flees a terrible disaster, a foreign invasion, a terrible famine and the association of non-devotees [of God] alone protects his life." – Sloka 3.19

"Scriptural lessons not put into practice are poison… but for an old man, a young woman is poison." – Sloka 4.15

"The guru who is lacking in knowledge must be forsaken. Reject also the frowning wife and relatives who have no affection." – Sloka 4.16

"The four ways of testing a man are through his renunciation, his character, his qualities and his actions." – Sloka 5.1

"Righteous conduct destroys misfortune, knowledge destroys ignorance, and circumspection destroys fear." – Sloka 5.11

"There is no disease equal to lust; there is no enemy equal to infatuation; and there is no fire like wrath. But there is no happiness higher than spiritual knowledge." – Sloka 5.12

"There is nothing as useless as trying to enlighten a dolt" – Sloka 5.16

"One is born alone and dies alone. Alone he experiences the good and bad consequences of his past deeds. Alone he is either sent to hell or to the supreme destination." – Sloka 5.13

"Swarga is but a straw to the man of spiritual knowledge. Life itself is but a straw to the man of courage. For the man of controlled senses, te beautiful female is a mere straw. And for someone who is detached, the entire universe is bur a straw." – Sloka 5.14

"By truth the Earth is sustained, by truth the sun shines, and truth causes Vayu the Wind God to blow. Verily all things rest upon truth." – Sloka 5.19

"And he who is bent upon gathering riches riches riches is blind to the evil of his ways." – Sloka 6.8

"… better to have no friend than to befriend a rascal; better to be without a disciple than have a stupid one; better to have no wife than a wicked one." – Sloka 6.11

"The one excellent lesson that should be learned from a lion is that whatever a man is set upon doing should be achieved with great vitality and effort." – Sloka 6.16

"A King's might is in the strength of his arms; the brahmanas power is in his spiritual knowledge; and a woman's power is in her comeliness, youth and sweetness." – Sloka 7.11 [The image below is of the famous King Chandragupta who defeated Alexander the Great]

"he whose wealth is enjoyment must abandon any quest for knowledge. He who values knowledge must not desire sense gratification." – Sri Canakya Niti, Sloka 10.3

"The empty-headed are never benefitted by instruction anymore than bamboo will become sandalwood by growing upon the slopes of the Malaya mountain" – Sri Canakya Niti, Sloka 10.8

"Diseases are nourished by sorrow, the body by milk [raw], senses by ghee, and flesh by meat." – Sri Canakya Niti, Sloka 10.20

"One should be cunning with those who are cunning, With a cheat behave like a cheat." – Sloka 12.3

"A wicked man may develop saintly qualities in the company of a devotee [of God], but a devotee does not become impious in the company of a wicked person. The Earth is scented by a flower that falls upon it, but the flower does not contract the odour of the Earth." – Sloka 12.7

"Truth is my mother and realised knowledge is my father, righteousness is my brother, mercy is my friend, inner peace is my wife, forgiveness si my son. These six are my kindsmen." – Sloka 12.11

".. death waits nearby. Therefore, immediately engage yourself in dharma" – Sloka 12.12

"Arjuna [Godly Vedic Warrior King] said "Brahmanas [Holy Vedic Sages] find joy in attending fasts, cows are delighted by chewing fresh grass, married ladies find pleasure in the company of their husbands; know o Bhagavan Krsna [God], that is the same way I rejoice in battle" – Sloka 12.13

"… the quarrelmonger, he who is disturbed in all spheres of his activities … are quickly ruined." – Sloka 12.18

"A life of only a moment is successful if that moment is spent in auspicious activities." – Sloka 13.1

"We should not worry about the past nor should we be anxious about the future; men of discernment deal only with the present moment." – Sloka 13.2

"He who is overly attached experiences fear and sorrow, for the root of all grief is attachment. Thus one should discard all attachment and be happy." – Sloka 13.5

"Since we come to this life naked and take nothing with us when we leave, those who fail to understand that wealth is meant for the service of the supreme Lord [God] will be crushed by it. And those who use the blessings of Laksmi [the Goddess of Wealth] in the service of her husband Lord Narayana are glorified." – Sloka 13.11 [Narayana is one of the Holy names of God described in the Vedic scriptures.]

"Who achieves all the pleasures that the mind desires? Everything is in the hands of providence. Therefore, one should learn contentment." – Sloka 13.13

"As a calf finds its mother among a thousand cows so the good or bad deeds of a man follow him." – Sloka 13.14

"Speak that which will please him from whom you expect a favour, just as the hunter sings sweetly to shoot the deer." – Sloka 14.9

"Always be cautious with fire, water, women, fools, serpents, and membes of the Royal family. Any of these six may cause death." – Sloka 14.11

"He is a pandita who speaks that which is suitable for the occasion; who renders loving service according to his ability; and who exhibits his anger no more than his ability to influence." – Sloka 14.14

"A single woman's body appears in the three different ways. To the yogi it is a corpse, to the lusty man it is a source of pleasure, to the dog it is a slab of flesh." – Sloka 14.15

"Eschew the company of the wicked and associate always with devotees [of God]. By day and night acquire virtue…" - Sloka 14.19

"There are two ways to deal with thorns and evil-minded men, either stomp them down with your shoes (so they cannot rise up again) or keep them at a safe distance." – Sloka 15.3

"True friendship means to act for others. To abstain from sin is true wisdom."- Sloka 15.8

"The Goddess of Fortune forsakes him who wears unclean garments, has dirty teeth, is a glutton, speaks harshly, and speaks from sunrise to sunset, even if he is Visnu [God] himself." – Sloka 15.4

"It is said that the Lord protects his brahmanas from acquiring the blessings of his wife Laksmi in the form of wealth, lest their heads become turned by excessive material attachment… and this is more important for one whose job is teaching society rather than becoming pre-occupied with wealth." – Sloka 15.16

"Fame is gained only by sufficient accumulation of punya [devotion to God]." – Sloka 15.18

"Those who wish to be celebrated in this temporary world are like the insignificant ant who longs to be king of the anthill."- Sloka 16.8

"The good qualities should characterise a man of discrimination, the brilliance of his qualities will be recognised just as a gem which is essentially bright really shines when fixed as an ornament of gold." – Sloka 16.9

"Death is preferable to a life of dishonor and infamy… disgrace brings grief day after day." – Sloka 16.16

"There are two nectarean fruits hanging from the poisonous tree of this world. The first is pleasant conversation and the second is the company of saintly men." – Sloka 16.18

"The favors of others should be repaid by acts of kindness. Likewise cruel behaviour may be returned with cruelty. There is no sinful reaction if a wicked fellow is renumerated in his own coin." – Sloka 17.2

"That which is distant, that which appears impossible, and that which is far beyond our reach can easily be brought into our hands by tapasya, for nothing can defeat religious austerity." – Sloka 17.3

"A woman robs a man of his vigor while [raw] milk restores it in an instant." – Sloka 17.14

"In this Kali-yuga [the current age of Chaos] there is no dearth of heartless people milling here and there waiting patiently to increase your misery (and anxiety). It is fruitless to seek sympathy from the materialist. Therefore, one must associate with genuine devotees [of God] to alleviate suffering caused by past karma." – Sloka 17.19 Commentary by Patita Pavana Dasa Adhikari

Divine Wisdom in the Ancient Vedic Scriptures

"If you open up your heart, You will know what I mean, We've been polluted so long, But here's a way for you to get clean, By chanting the name of the Lord and You'll be free, The Lord is awaiting on you all to awaken And see" – George Harrison, the world famous member of the band The Beatles, from the song 'Awaiting on you All'

"the big difference between Vedic science and Western science is in the Vedas we get the information that everything is going on under the direction of intelligent management. There is no chance. There is a good reason for everything that is happening in the universe and there is intelligence behind the scenes managing and directing everything." - Madhudvisa dasa, Author

"The Vedas are the most rewarding and uplifting reading that is possible in the world." - Arthur Schopenhauer

"[The Bhagavad Gita] is the best of books… Were I a preacher, I would venture sometimes to take from its texts the motto and moral of my discourse. It would be healthful and invigorating to breathe some of this mountain air into the lungs of Christendom." – Amos Bronson Alcott (1799-1888) writer, philosopher, visionary

"The glory of the Vedic wisdom was seen in the caliber of its followers. When we become devoted to God, we become godly. This was the basis of the theistic Vedic social order. Moreover, another cardinal principle was: real human progress is measured not by the development of technological faculties, but by the development of spiritual qualities." – Chaitanya Charan das, Author of Science and Spirituality

"Whenever I have read any part of the Vedas, I have felt that some unearthly and unknown light illuminated me. I the great teachings of the Vedas, there is no touch of sectarianism. It is of all ages, climbs, and nationalities and is the royal road for the attainment of the Great Knowledge." – Henry David Thoreau, American Writer and Philosopher

"The wisdom, insight and knowledge of the Vedic scriptures enable every human to follow his path toward spiritual development and to achieve complete physical, emotional and interpersonal wellbeing. The Vedic way is not a religion it can be followed by peoples of all faiths." - Marcus Schmieke, Author

"One should not think that this chanting or mantra is a sectarian affair, that Visnu or Krishna is the name of a 'Hindu' God, and is not the name of 'our' God. By definition there can only be one God, however he may be known differently through different religions." - Dhanesvara dasa, Author

"Krishna wants to emphasise that the best material knowledge... cannot compare to pure knowledge of the soul... knowledge of temporary material affairs, can never supplant authoritative spiritual science. We have an eternal spiritual identity different from the body and the mind... we can start to experience the existence and power of our nonmaterial self, the soul. This is where real freedom begins... No amount of altering material nature – no material construction, deconstruction, or reconstruction – can ultimately satisfy the individual or society, because our real problem is disconnection from the Supreme... Therefore we have to engage ourselves in occupational engagements that will evoke our divine consciousness Srimad Bhagavatam (1.2.8)" - Devamrita Swami, Author

"We need transcendental knowledge – intelligence beyond the material – to inform us. Then we can understand the true and full potential of the human being. Blind to our true nature we become easy prey for manipulation, both the external demands of the socio-political schemes of our so-called 'leaders' and by the internal, though artificially induced, desires of our own contaminated minds." – Devamrita Swami, Author

"... when a boy wants to develop a loving relationship with a girl, he very carefully does the things that will please her and he scrupulously avoids the things that will displease her. The same principle holds true in spiritual life, wherein an aspiring transcendentalist desires to develop a loving relationship with Krishna (God)" – Chaitanya Charan das, Author of Spiritual Scientist, pg 105

"Self-deception means accepting the illusion of becoming powerful, self-sufficient and content outside the harmony of the Whole (God). Those who have such a separatist mentality are unable to see their spiritual individuality... Having cut themselves off from the Source, they no longer obtain their life energy from there. Consequently, they start to exploit the energy of other beings – animal, plants, human beings and the planet itself." – Dhanesvara das, Author

"Our happiness and satisfaction are to be found in developing our relationship of eternal love with the One who will give us unconditional unending love in return.… Live as you were meant to live and act for the highest achievement that human life has to offer – your spiritual emancipation – and at the same time be genuinely happy in this world." – Dhanesvara das, Author

The following quotes are from the writings, talks and translations of the Vedas by His Divine Grace A. C Bhaktivedanta Swami Srila Prabhupada. Srila Prabhupada (1896 – 1977) is a famous spiritual, philosophical, and religious personality from India who spread the 'Hare Krishna' mantra (a mantra of devotion to God) and the teachings of Vedic Vaishnavism (devotion of God) to the world. He is regarded as a great saint and representative of God in the tradition of Vedic Vaishnavism.

"We always see that life comes life... we have never seen life come from dead matter. Doesn't that suggest the origin of life is life and not matter?" – Srila Prabhupada

"Life's desires should never be aimed at gratifying the senses. One should desire to live only because human life enables one to inquire about the Absolute Truth. This should be the goal of all works." – Srimad Bhagavatam Text 10 (Canto l, Ch. 2) Translation by Srila Prabhupada

"Do not waste even a second of your life. A single moment which has been wasted cannot be purchased back for ten thousand gold coins. He who wastes his life for no profit becomes the greatest loser." - Srila Prabhupada

"It is only by one's behaviour by which one can understand who is our friend and who is our enemy. Similarly, just as we deal with ordinary daily affairs I have my own dealings with myself. If I deal with myself as a friend, then I am my friend. And if I deal with myself inimically… then what is that – friendship or enmity?... I have to get myself out of the entanglement of this material nature. If I act in that way, then I am my friend… If I do not act I that way, then I am my enemy. So I am either my own friend or I am my own enemy." - Srila Prabhupada

"at the present moment, the modern civilization on the basis of so-called scientific knowledge and economic development is trying to avoid God consciousness, or Krishna Consciousness—that is the defect of the modern civilization. Therefore, in spite of all advancement it is zero. So zero has no value. And millions of zeros put together does not make any value. But one is put on the left side of the zero, it increases the value. Then one zero becomes 10, two zero becomes 100, three zero becomes 1000, so it is very nice. This point should be clearly discussed, that without God consciousness, Krishna Consciousness, any attempt of human civilization so-called philosophical or political or economical or labor, they are all zeros." – Srila Prabhupada

"Shape your life so you are always conscious of Me. Offer all your love, endeavours and reverence to Me. Surely, in pure yoga you will reunite with Me. I promise you this because you're my own intimate part, My beloved, My very dear friend. " – Bhagavad Gita As It Is (18.64), Translation by Srila Prabhupada

"A person who has no mother at home and whose wife is not agreeable with him should immediately renounce his family life and go away to the forest. For such a person, living at home and living in the forest are equal." - Srila Prabhupada

"Human beings must engage in pious activities, not sinful activities. Otherwise they have no brain. They are no better than animals… Today practically no one is making this distinction… You may create hundreds of organisations, but society will never be happy. That is the verdict…. If society does not know what is sinful and what is pious, it is all useless." – Srila Prabhupada

"An evil man should be avoided, even though he may be decorated with great knowledge. He is just like a venomous serpent adorned with a jewel on his hood. Is not such a snake fearful?... Then if someone thinks 'Oh here is a snake with a jewel, let me embrace him.' No, no, no, it is very ferocious. Even if a jewel is there, it is ferocious."- Srila Prabhupada

"..their (material) reality is a dog's race, and our reality is to advance in self-realization, Krsna consciousness….In the Vedic system people are not lazy they are busy working for a higher purpose." – Srila Prabhupada

"The duration of one's life in the material world may end at any moment, but if within this life one does something worthy, that qualification is depicted in history eterneally." – Srimad Bhagavatam 9.13.3, Translation by Srila Prabhupada

"The main thing is, society must learn to discriminate between pious and sinful activities. Human beings must engage in pious activities, not sinful activities. Otherwise, they have no brain. They are no better than animals... Today practically no one is making this distinction... This mean society has no brain. You may create hundreds of organisations, but society will never be happy. That is the verdict.... If society does not know what is sinful and what is pious, it is all useless." - Srila Prabhupada

"Human prosperity flourishes by natural gifts and not by gigantic industrial enterprises, which are the products of a godless civilisation and cause the destruction of the noble aims of human life" - Srila Prabhupada

"Human energy should be properly utilised in developing the finer senses for spiritual understanding. " – Srila Prabhupada

"Although demons have created many plans for industry and hard labor so that people will work day and night like animals, this is not the purpose of civilization.... One should not endeavor for ugra-karma, or unnecessary work for sense gratification... For flickering happiness, people waste their human energy, not understanding the importance of the Krsna consciousness movement..." – from purport on Srimad Bhagavatam 9.24.59, Translation by Srila Prabhupada

The Goddess Saraswati – the Goddess of Creativity, Art, Knowledge and Learning in Vedic Literature

Saraswati (Sanskrit: सरस्वती), also spelled as Sarasvati, is described in the ancient Vedic literatures as the goddess of knowledge, music, flowing water, abundance and wealth, art, speech, wisdom, and learning. She is a also revered in Jainism and Buddhism. She has remained significant as a goddess from the Vedic period through the modern period. She is generally depicted with four arms (which hold four symbols: a book, a rosary, a water pot, and a musical instrument called the veena).

Her importance grows in the later Vedas composed after the Rigveda as well as in the later Brahmana texts, and the word evolves in its meaning from "waters that purify", to "that which purifies", to "vach (speech) that purifies", to "knowledge that purifies", and ultimately into a spiritual concept of a goddess that embodies knowledge, arts, music, melody, muse, language, rhetoric, eloquence, creative work and anything whose flow purifies the essence and self of a person.

Sarasvati is known by many names. Some examples of synonyms for Sarasvati include Brahmani (power of Brahma), Brahmi (goddess of sciences), Bharadi (goddess of history), Vani and Vachi (both referring to the flow of music/song, melodious speech, eloquent speaking respectively), Varnesvari (goddess of letters), Kavijihvagravasini (one who dwells on the tongue of poets).

She is praised in the Vedas as a water goddess of purification, while in the Dharmashastras, Saraswati is invoked to remind the reader to meditate on virtue, and on the meaning (artha) of one's actions (karma).

Saraswati first appears in the Rigveda, the most ancient source of the Vedic religion. Sarawsati holds significant religious and symbolic value in the Rigveda, as a deified entity embodying attributes of abundance and power. Primarily linked with the celestial domain of Waters (Apas) and the formidable Storm Gods (Maruts), this deity forms an integral triadic association alongside the sacrificial goddesses Ila and Bharati within the pantheon. Saraswati is described as a loud and powerful flood who roars like a bull and cannot be controlled.

If you wish to be blessed with creativity and wisdom and spiritual purification one can say a prayer of devotion. Fold your hands in sincere devotion and sincerely chant or sing: "All Glories to Goddess Sarasvati".

If you wish to say a prayer in the Sanskrit language, the Saraswati Shloka is a hymn is composed of the following two verses:

> sarasvatī namastubhyaṃ varade kāmarūpiṇī
> vidyārambhaṃ kariṣyāmi siddhirbhavatu me sadā

> Translation: O Saraswati; salutations to you; you who offers boons; you who takes the form of desires. As I begin my studies, may there always be accomplishment for me.